TOOLS FOR CAREGIVERS

- **F&P LEVEL:** B
- **WORD COUNT:** 24
- **CURRICULUM CONNECTIONS:** animals, habitats, nature

Skills to Teach

- **HIGH-FREQUENCY WORDS:** a, has, it
- **CONTENT WORDS:** eyes, fins, gills, shark, snout, swims, tail, teeth
- **PUNCTUATION:** periods
- **WORD STUDY:** digraph *sh* (*shark*); long /a/, spelled *ai* (*tail*); long /e/, spelled *ee* (*teeth*); /ow/, spelled *ou* (*snout*)
- **TEXT TYPE:** information report

Before Reading Activities

- Read the title and give a simple statement of the main idea.
- Have students "walk" through the book and talk about what they see in the pictures.
- Introduce new vocabulary by having students predict the first letter and locate the word in the text.
- Discuss any unfamiliar concepts that are in the text.

After Reading Activities

Flip back through the book with readers and note the images. There are different kinds of sharks in the book. Can readers name them? For example, there is a hammerhead shark on pages 8–9 and a great white shark on page 11. Ask readers to name what all of the sharks have in common.

Tadpole Books are published by Jump!, 5357 Penn Avenue South, Minneapolis, MN 55419, www.jumplibrary.com

Copyright ©2024 Jump!. International copyright reserved in all countries. No part of this book may be reproduced in any form without written permission from the publisher.

Editor: Jenna Gleisner **Designer:** Emma Almgren-Bersie

Photo Credits: Konstantin Novikov/Shutterstock, cover; frantisekhojdysz/Shutterstock, 1; EXTREME-PHOTOGRAPHER/iStock, 2tl, 8–9; Beto Bormann/iStock, 2tr, 4–5; Hannes Klostermann/Alamy, 2ml, 12–13; Tomas Kotouc/Shutterstock, 2mr, 14–15; Howard Chen/iStock, 2bl, 6–7; Nature Picture Library/Alamy, 2br, 10–11; Jsegalexplore/Shutterstock, 3; Oleg Kovtun Hydrobio/Shutterstock, 16fl; SaltedLife/Shutterstock, 16tr; Jesus Cobaleda/Shutterstock, 16bl; Katerina Maksymenko/Shutterstock, 16br.

Library of Congress Cataloging-in-Publication Data
Names: Deniston, Natalie, author.
Title: Sharks / by Natalie Deniston.
Description: Minneapolis, MN: Jump!, Inc. [2024]
Series: My first animal books | Includes index.
Audience: Ages 3–6
Identifiers: LCCN 2023023786 (print)
LCCN 2023023787 (ebook)
ISBN 9798889965862 (hardcover)
ISBN 9798889965879 (paperback)
ISBN 9798889965886 (ebook)
Subjects: LCSH: Sharks—Juvenile literature.
Classification: LCC QL638.9 .D456 2024 (print)
LCC QL638.9 (ebook)
DDC 597.3—dc23/eng/20230522
LC record available at https://lccn.loc.gov/2023023786
LC ebook record available at https://lccn.loc.gov/2023023787

MY FIRST ANIMAL BOOKS

SHARKS

by Natalie Deniston

TABLE OF CONTENTS

Words to Know............................2

Sharks....................................3

Let's Review!............................16

Index....................................16

WORDS TO KNOW

eyes

fins

gills

snout

tail

teeth

SHARKS

A shark swims.

It has fins.

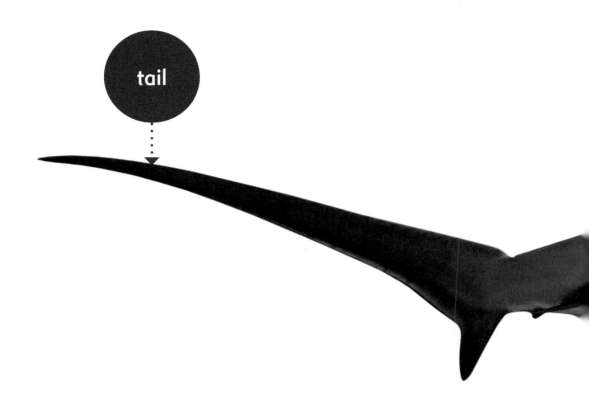

It has a tail.

eye

It has eyes.

tooth

It has teeth.

LET'S REVIEW!

Sharks are fish. They swim in the ocean. They breathe with gills. Point to the other kinds of fish you see below.

INDEX

eyes 9
fins 5
gills 13
snout 15

swims 3
tail 7
teeth 11